MW01593661

Jesus for Our Time

J. Ellsworth Kalas

Abingdon Press
Nashville

JESUS FOR OUR TIME

Copyright © 1997 by Abingdon Press

This book is printed on acid-free, recycled paper.

ISBN 0-687-05119-3

97 98 99 00 01 02 03 04 05 06 — 10 9 8 7 6 5 4 3 2 1

MANUFACTURED IN THE UNITED STATES OF AMERICA

Contents

Introduction

Biblical scholars always seem to be searching for the historical Jesus. Their quest is a worthy one, and at times we profit from it. But most of us day-by-day believers have a different question. We're looking for a twentieth-century Jesus; we wonder what Jesus would be like if he were physically present with us today.

Our question is more than idle curiosity. Yes, of course it's fun to imagine how Jesus might live in a world of computers, jet planes, and universities that are larger than many ancient cities. But we're really looking at a much bigger question. If Jesus is the Savior of the world, as many of us believe and as the church has always taught, then how does he relate to the kind of world in which we live? Jesus is sometimes described as "the Man for all times." How, then, does he fit in *our* times? What kind of person would he be if he were a resident of Dallas or Oskaloosa, of Alabama or Colorado? The people in first-century Galilee and Judea knew him in the normal context of their daily lives; what might he be like in our time and place?

As you read the chapters that follow, you will see that I have put some boundaries around my imagination. I haven't chosen, for example, to picture Jesus as a computer specialist or an airplane pilot, even though those occupations are significant, and typical of our times. I have chosen rather to imagine Jesus in roles for which there are rather clear parallels in the Gospel records. Perhaps some highly imaginative person might find some New Testament lifestyle that might be projected to resemble an electrical engineer, a pilot, or a professional athlete, but the connection would have more to do with novelty than with enlightenment.

But this isn't to say that you will automatically feel good about the seven roles I have chosen. You may find it relatively easy to imagine Jesus as a modern physician, but be stumbled by the picture of Jesus as a humorist or as a business executive. Yet I find it easy to infer each of these roles from the data the Gospel writers have given us, and I'm satisfied that if you will enter the stories with me, you will find the possibilities I have described. But even if some picture does not appeal to you, I hope you will learn from it.

Above all, I hope that by the time you have finished these seven brief chapters you will feel you know Jesus Christ better, and that you will love him more deeply. And while that is happening, I pray that you will discover new inner resources for following Jesus Christ in our time. He is our example as well as our Savior, so it is always the goal of the Christian life to be Christlike in the time in which we live. By the grace of God, may it be so for you and for me.

J. Ellsworth Kalas

Jesus of Nazareth, M.D.

Scripture Lesson: Luke 5:17-26

W e often call Jesus "the Great Physician," but I doubt that we use the term in a modern sense. We picture a compassionate first-century figure, working in a world where—as we perceive it—medicine was so primitive that faith and miracles were the only hope people had.

But first-century medicine in Palestine probably wasn't as primitive as we are inclined to think. We should remember, for instance, that medicine still pledges itself to an oath developed by the Greek physician, Hippocrates, more than four hundred years before Christ. As for Jesus, he grew up among a people whose practices of sanitation and hygiene were often well in advance of practices in our Western world until into the mid-nineteenth century. Jewish law in the first century required that every town have either a physician and a surgeon, or at least one physician who was also qualified to act as a surgeon. These medical people were licensed by the rabbis, who were themselves students of medicine and hygiene. Some records suggest that Jewish surgeons even knew how to operate for cataracts. True, the people of Jesus' time didn't have such sophisticated medical procedures as X-rays, organ transplants, kidney dialysis, or chemotherapy, but they knew more about the fundamentals than we usually assume, and many of their instruments and medicines were surprisingly similar to those we employ today.

Perhaps thinking of Jesus as a modern-day physician makes you uneasy on a different level. A doctor has to follow a prescribed course of education, and you can't imagine Jesus going to college and medical school. Why not? Without a doubt Jesus went through the standard educational pattern of his day, attending village rabbinical schools. And remember that when John the Baptist objected to baptizing Jesus, because he wasn't worthy to do so, Jesus made clear that he would pass through all the requirements of righteousness (Matt. 3:15). I venture that if Jesus lived in the twentieth century, he would bring himself under the regulations of the times.

Yes, if Jesus were here today, I believe he would be a physician. As surely as he healed the sick nineteen centuries ago, he would heal them today. No doubt his healings would depend more upon direct divine intervention than upon our customary methods; yet I think he would use what the times and opportunities provided. His concern would not be method, but the relieving of human misery. Let me tell you the kind of physician I think he would be.

It is often said that medicine is both an art and a science. It is, of course, a science, in which certain chemicals, treatments, and procedures are expected to bring particular results. But medicine isn't simply a science, because we humans are much too complex for rigid analysis. The best physicians possess some of the qualities of a poet or a painter; a patient's symptoms are rarely so clear as to fit purely scientific diagnoses. And even after treatment begins, drugs and surgery are only part of the answer. Medicine also calls for art—intangible qualities in the person of the physician—and perhaps even more often, in the person of the nurse.

Judging from what happened nineteen centuries ago, if Jesus of Nazareth were a physician today, he would practice the medicine of *compassion*. That mood characterizes the Gospel records. "When he saw the crowds," Matthew said, "he had compassion for them, because they were harassed and helpless" (Matt. 9:36). It is impossible to grasp the nature of Jesus' healing ministry unless we remember his quality of compassion.

I think especially of an instance Mark reports. A leper came to Jesus for healing. In those days the fear of leprosy was so great that the law required that one stay many feet away from anyone so afflicted, and lepers were required to announce their condition to prevent contact. But when Jesus saw this man's need, he was "moved with pity" (Mark 1:41). Then Jesus violated the laws of distance and of isolation. He reached out his hand and touched the leper, making him well. Here was compassion in action. It was not just a kindly feeling of sympathy, but a quality that walked into the other person's need and made it his own.

If Jesus were a physician today, he would practice medicine not only with compassion, but also with *authority*. Several years ago a physician friend introduced me to a nineteenth-century medical textbook that offered a list of the qualities essential to being a good physician. The word that caught my friend's attention was *dogmatic;* a good physician, the professor said, must be dogmatic.

That isn't a term we ordinarily associate with medicine, but I think I see the point: A doctor must speak with a ring of certainty. There must be authority in his or her manner. This does not mean that we want our doctor to pretend to know more than he or she actually knows, but when the doctor speaks, we like to feel that he or she is confident about what is being said. I see this quality in Jesus. Think of the time he came upon a man with a withered hand. We are told that Jesus said, "Stretch out your hand" (Mark 3:5). What an order to give a person with a helpless, drooping arm! The command might almost seem heartless. But Jesus spoke with such assurance, such obvious command of the situation, that the man stretched out his arm until the limp, helpless limb became an instrument of strength.

The New Testament often uses a term that upsets our twentieth-century minds: demons. In cases of mental illness and in some instances of persons who were deaf and mute, Jesus commanded evil spirits to come out of the persons. Without getting into a full-blown theological discussion of demons, let me simply note that in these instances we see Jesus in command. There is, indeed, some monstrous evil in the universe that shows itself in the agonies of our world, whether in withered limbs and malignancies, or in war and seething prejudice. Jesus looked at such manifestations and saw beyond the immediate instance to the power of evil that they manifested, and with magnificent authority he commanded an end to the reign of illness in such persons.

In some cases, people were so moved by the power they saw in Jesus that they didn't even ask for healing; they simply got near enough to touch a fringe of his garments, and they were healed (Mark 6:56). I think Jesus would evoke such feelings in many of us. If we were to come into his office today, or if he were to come into our hospital room, some of us would say at the very sight of him, "All is well! Don't bother with a prescription!"

There is also a sense in which Jesus might sometimes frighten some of us, because he would practice medicine in a *radical* way. I use the word in its basic sense: he would get at the root of things. And sometimes, in getting at the root of our lives, he might reveal to us things we'd rather not know about ourselves. I'm sure that was the case with the man Jesus healed at the pool of Bethesda. One has the feeling that the man had come to enjoy his sickness and the pity it brought him. Jesus pierced through to the heart of his need when he asked, "Do you want to be made well?" (John 5:6).

Often Jesus healed the spirit even as he healed the body. Consider the story in Luke 5. Several men brought a paralyzed man to Jesus in search of healing. But before Jesus even considered the man's obvious physical need, he said, "Friend, your sins are forgiven you" (Luke 5:20). I'm very sure the man's sense of guilt was preventing his being healed. In those days it was commonly taught and believed that all sickness was a result of sin. This paralyzed man must have been under a great burden of guilt, much of it imposed on him by others. If Jesus had healed him without first giving him forgiveness, it would have been only a matter of time before another illness would have settled upon him. Indeed, I doubt that the initial healing could have taken place if there had not first been this deliverance from sin and guilt.

Dr. Paul Tournier, the Swiss physician and author, says that any kind of illness raises questions of two distinct kinds. The first is scientific, which concerns the nature of the illness and its mechanism. The second is spiritual, with questions concerning the deep meaning of the illness. So it is, Tournier continues, that each illness needs two diagnoses, a scientific one and a spiritual one. If the physician treats only the physical or mechanistic side of the illness, there cannot be a complete healing. Tournier remembers how a French doctor once began an address to a congress of doctors by quoting one of his patients: "We are prevented from dying; we are not helped to live." That is to say—we need *radical* healing. We need not simply a cure for our ulcer, our migraine, our arthritis; we need a deep wellspring of health. Many people who are not measurably ill are yet in no sense truly healthy. Radical healing is needed.

So perhaps another word should be used to describe the kind of medicine Jesus of Nazareth would practice today: *preventive* medicine. Every worthy physician wishes he or she might help patients form such habits and establish such an outlook on life as would prevent many illnesses. Jesus was such a physician.

We need Jesus of Nazareth, M.D. As wonderfully as science has progressed and as much as medical care has improved, we still need one who can provide radical, deep-down healing—the kind that involves soul as well as body. Even with some 684,000 physicians in the United States alone, we need one more: The Man of Galilee.

Study Questions

1. Does it detract from your sense of the divinity of Jesus to think of him going to college or medical school today? Why do you think it is easier for most of us to think of him being trained by the village rabbi? What issues of faith keep us from imagining Jesus as part of our modern world?
2. Read Matthew 9:36. How would you define compassion as it is demonstrated in the ministry of Jesus? Whom do you know who seems to manifest compassion? What is it about this person that makes you feel she or he is compassionate?
3. Read Mark 3:1-5. How is it that Jesus could speak with such authority? We read that sometimes Jesus was unable to heal because of the person's unbelief (see Mark 6:5, 6). Why might the man with the withered hand have had faith when some others did not?
4. Read Luke 5:17-26. Have you known persons who seemed to prefer sickness to health? When have you, as a child or an adult, been guilty, even briefly, of such an attitude? How did your attitude affect the healing process?

5. List some "emotional secrets" of healthy living. If this is difficult for you, ask a friend who exhibits both physical and spiritual health.

Focus for the Week:
Lent Is a Time of Healing

During the Lenten season, there can be a two-fold ministry of healing. In the process of our own deeper disciplines of faith, so appropriate to this season, we are made more open to healing. It is right that we should come to God with our physical, emotional, and spiritual pains; then, we should become channels of healing kindness to others who are suffering.

In what ways you do seek God's healing? How can you be a channel of healing to others this week?

Jesus of Nazareth, News Analyst

Scripture Lesson: Matthew 24:32-44

No other generation in human history has had such a love affair with the news as has ours. Of course no other generation has had so much news to report, because we live in a world of constant change. Nor has any previous generation had such facilities for getting the news into our hands while it is still news. As a result, we have become the news-generation. Mind you, we complain constantly about the news media; few subjects irritate people more than the way the media do their job. But we keep on tuning in the evening news, and we continue to subscribe to newspapers, news magazines, and journals of opinion. Perhaps the irritation we feel only indicates how much the news means to us. Even our anger with the media is a love/hate relationship, as indicated by the fact that during presidential conventions, more people seek autographs from the network news personalities than from the presidential candidates.

Although the printing press, radio, television, and the Internet have made news more immediately accessible, the love of news is nothing new. In the first-century world, the Romans had an institution that was known as the *album*. This wasn't a book, as the name would suggest today, but a tablet or noticeboard that was set up in a public place in Rome where everyone could study its contents. We don't know if the Romans had something of this sort in outposts of their empire, such as Jerusalem, but it seems likely. After all, the emperor wanted to get information into the hands of all the citizens and here was a way to do so. And in Jerusalem itself there was a sort of news sheet that was circulated regularly, whether through the Roman government or the high priests. In any event, I think I can safely say that when two first-century people met on a corner in Jerusalem or Nazareth, they probably said, "What's new?"

Today we're curious not only to hear the news, we also want to know what it means. We want someone to analyze it, so we can get at its perhaps hidden significance. The surface story may be interesting, but we wonder what's behind it. And we also wonder what kind of selection the reporters may have made in the facts they choose to pass along to us, and those they choose to omit. We wish someone could predict with certainty the possibilities of world peace, or which way the economy is going, or what will happen if a given person is elected to office.

So we're always looking for a news analyst. Although most of us will confess that we tend to read those columnists and those magazines or journals that reflect our own prejudices, we also wish we might find some analyst who would report with absolute integrity. Even if his or her position didn't always coincide with our own, we'd like to know what such a person thinks. And especially, we wish that our analyst would not only interpret the news, but could somehow also shape and influence it for good.

If Jesus of Nazareth were physically present with us today, I think he might be such a news analyst. Nearly twenty centuries ago the Gospel writers reported that Jesus looked at the multitude and observed they were like sheep without a shepherd (Matt. 9:36; Mark 6:34)—poor confused creatures, wandering aimlessly and at last, tragically. I think he would have the same reaction today, in this world where many people not only hover over newspaper, television, and radio, but also turn to a psychic or an astrologer to see if they can make sense of it all. We are indeed sheep without a shepherd. We need someone who can tell us, "Here's the meaning of it all, and here's what you should do about it."

In truth, Jesus grew up in a culture where the news analyst was a respected figure. But they didn't call them news analysts; they called them prophets. Incidentally, the people responded to them with the same love/hate relationship that we have today with the news media—only more so, because they often persecuted and killed the prophets. And although Israel hadn't had a notable prophet for several centuries before Jesus' birth, the people continued to read the earlier prophets with great faithfulness, still seeking guidance from their writings.

By reading the writings of these prophets, these ancient news analysts, the people developed a certain attitude toward national and world events. It was the prophets' deep, absolute conviction that God is at work in the affairs of the human race—and therefore, that the decisions we make, as individuals and as nations, are ultimately moral decisions, decisions of right and wrong. God is an issue in all our decisions, whether we recognize it to be so or not.

This, of course, was the point of view from which Jesus interpreted the news of the day—or, if you wish, the news of the ages. Each day is, after all, a piece of the ages; written smaller, but more significant because we must read it "up close." So if Jesus were our news analyst, he would bring each issue of the day into a moral compass. He would cut through our usual expediencies, moving fearlessly to the heart of the matter, right and wrong. In doing so, he would startle most of us. We have grown so accustomed to reading issues through the spectacles of economics, or national pride, or ethnic prejudice, or personal advantage that we cannot imagine having all of these stripped away. Mind you, most of us mean well, but we have become captives to our culture and its mores. If Jesus were to do a nightly analysis of our news, I wonder how long it would be before we would crucify him again?

What would Jesus tell us about the future? We want our pundits to give us a head start on next week, next football game, next election. Indeed, we've made a science of it; the pollsters can tell us who will win the next election, and a computer can tell us, on the basis of strength of schedule, who will win the football game. But these are all preliminary matters. What about the ultimate future, the goal toward which history is moving?

The disciples came to Jesus with that kind of question. They wanted to know about the future of Jerusalem, and about the end of all things. Jesus gave a wide-ranging answer, then summed up matters by comparing the end times with the days of Noah. In Noah's day, Jesus said, people were eating and drinking, marrying and giving in marriage (Matt. 24:38, 39)—that is, life was going on at a perfectly normal pace. Eating and drinking, marrying and giving in marriage—these activities are the essence of life as routine. And that was the catch—everything was so routine that the flood caught them by surprise. So it will be at the end, Jesus said.

So what is the secret? Quite simple: *always be ready* (Matt. 24:44). Live each day as if it were the consummation of all things.

On the one hand, such advice is the best kind of common sense; since we don't know what today, or any day, will bring, let us always be prepared for the ultimate. By doing so, we are ready for every day; no day will take us by surprise. And there's also a certain grandeur in this kind of living, because by such an outlook we lift every day to a level of ultimacy. Come to think of it, we should—because every day, in its own right and dimension, *is* ultimate.

So there's a sense in which Jesus would say, Don't worry about the headlines! Sufficient to the day is the headline thereof (Matt. 6:34). He would not have us be held captive to the fears of the day, the frightening prognostications, the whinings of the pollsters. Each day has its own divine fullness, its eternal potential; glory in it, and leave the rest to God.

But suppose disaster comes? What if the threat of disaster becomes reality? What if another war breaks out? What if the thin veneer of civilization is stripped away and our world shows itself to be hardly a step from savagery? Suppose, even, that the fragile experiment of democracy should end in some new totalitarianism? What then? I think that Jesus, the News Analyst, would tell us to lift up our heads, knowing that our redemption is very near (Luke 21:28). Jesus' analysis of the future is always immersed in hope, because he knows the One to whom the future belongs. The future will end with neither a bang nor a whimper, but with a shout of triumph. God will see to that.

What a news analyst he would be, this Jesus of Nazareth! He would know that what happens is not simply one fool thing after another, even if those of us who put the events together sometimes do so in foolish fashion. He would be utterly certain that our heavenly Father is at work behind the scenes, back of the headline events, bringing order out of what might otherwise be misshapen and destructive. He would be enough of a realist to know that disaster can indeed come, and to warn us of the conduct that will lead to disaster. But he would also tell us how to avoid disaster, or how to remake our world—both public and private—when disaster has left it in hopelessness.

But I will not mourn that Jesus of Nazareth is not our turn-of-the-century news analyst. Why should I mourn, when he has left behind quite clear words for each day? I think I can hear him say, "Don't be afraid. I have overcome the world. The headlines may change, but I remain."

Study Questions

1. Why are we so often irritated by the news media? How, specifically, should a Christian relate to the media coverage of news?
2. Is there anything in our culture that you think might be compared to the Old Testament prophets?
3. Consider this familiar hypothetical question: What would you do today if you knew Jesus were returning by nightfall? Any specific issues you would resolve? Any persons to whom you would make amends? Any special attention to matters of your own soul?
4. Who might employ Jesus as a news analyst in our day? Would you listen to him? How would you respond if he contradicted your party line?
5. What secrets have you learned about maintaining your inner poise in a culture like ours, which seems to be swept by so many passing moods?

Focus for the Week: Analyzing Our Culture

Lent has traditionally been a season for analyzing our personal relationship to our culture. For many this has to do with personal matters of diet and conduct. But what about such highly significant matters as our "intellectual diet"—the periodicals and books we read and the programs we watch or to which we listen, which then shape our outlook on life? This is a good season for analyzing the news of our own souls, and the way we're preparing these souls for our continuing pilgrimage.

What changes do you need to make in your "intellectual diet" this season?

Jesus of Nazareth, Humorist

Scripture Lesson: Matthew 6:31–7:5

We don't usually think of Jesus as a humorist, and that's too bad, because it suggests that we think humor is something unworthy of Jesus. In thinking that way, we make life dramatically "smaller," and we make Jesus less than the New Testament portrays him to be.

Consider for a moment how big a part humor plays in life. I'm not speaking simply about those paid comedians who sometimes become multimillionaires by making us laugh, or the thousands of persons who write the scripts for comedians and comedies. And I'm looking beyond the comic strips that are part of nearly every newspaper, the humor columnist, the circus clown, the mime, and the ventriloquist, all of whom depend on our sense of humor. I'm thinking of the way humor lubricates daily life. Whether in the familiar repartee of coworkers, the daily exchange of the server and the regular patron in a small-town restaurant, or the comments of the person sitting behind you at the baseball game, humor makes our days. No wonder, then, that women say a sense of humor is more important than money when choosing the man they marry; and no wonder that few insults hurt more than "You just don't have a sense of humor."

Well, Jesus had a sense of humor, and he demonstrated it daily. Somehow we have become so taken with his weeping at the tomb of Lazarus and of his sorrow over the city of Jerusalem that we forget the far more frequent instances when he evoked laughter among those who heard him. After all, people didn't invite him to their dinner parties because he brought sadness with him; and whatever the exaggeration when his enemies accused him of being a winebibber and a glutton, they obviously were building on something in Jesus' reputation for being a person of social hilarity. When Jesus said that he had come so that we might have life more abundant, he couldn't have got away with it if he had looked like a walking advertisement for dyspepsia.

Nearly a generation ago, the late Quaker theologian Elton Trueblood wrote a book about the humor of Jesus. The idea was first planted in his mind when he was reading to his four-year-old son from the seventh chapter of Matthew's Gospel, where Jesus said, "Why do you see the speck in your neighbor's eye, but do not notice the log in your own eye?" (v. 3). The little boy suddenly began to laugh. He saw how funny the passage was, and because no one had yet conditioned his mind to be somber about Jesus, he naturally broke into laughter (*The Humor of Christ*, 9).

The reason most of us are uncomfortable with Jesus as a humorist is because in our minds we have an image of an unsmiling Savior. This is partly because we have different definitions and styles of humor. Virginia Woolf said that humor is "the first of the gifts to perish in a foreign tongue." What evokes laughter in one ethnic group, age, or culture may only bring bewilderment in another. In first-century Palestine, exaggeration was a favorite form of humor, and Jesus used it well. The Pharisees were so cautious about what they drank that they carried a bit of cloth to strain any foreign substance from beverages. One day Jesus drew upon this practice to chide the Pharisees about the way they handled their money. They were so meticulous about tithing that they measured out the tithe on a few ounces of spices, but they played fast and loose with the widows' houses on which they held mortgages—what Jesus called "the weightier matters of the law." You strain out the gnat, Jesus said, and swallow the camel (Matt. 23:23, 24).

Everyone in the crowd got the picture. They imagined a Pharisee triumphantly catching a gnat in his little square of cloth, then solemnly proceeding to swallow a camel. As Jesus spoke, with a wry grin, they pictured those pawed feet going down, that disdainful head, the neck and the massive hump, the hindquarters and the back legs—and with it all, not even a moment of protest on the face of the Pharisee!

As we see in the passage from the seventh chapter of Matthew, Jesus also used exaggeration to attack hypocrisy. It's an absurd scene: a friend approaches you, a black patch covering each eye, and volunteers to remove a speck in your eye. You pull back in horror. "Don't touch my eye! Not until you can see properly." But so often we try to repair other people's lives when our spiritual vision is thoroughly distorted by our own sins and shortcomings.

Jesus aimed many of his barbs of humor at the superpious. And rightly so, because no one is more ridiculous than the person who tries to impress others with his or her religiosity. In Jesus' day the painfully pious would sprinkle ashes over the body and leave the face unwashed so others would know they were fasting. And of course they would look appropriately distressed. Jesus must have had a twinkle in his eye when he said that these folks already had their reward because they had got the attention they wanted. Then he said that when you fast you should anoint your head and wash your face, so no one but God will guess that you are fasting (Matt. 6:16-18). He was saying, "If you plan to fast, take a good shower or bath (don't forget the bath salts!), put on some perfume or aftershave, and stride down the street as if you're going to a party. People will never guess that you're fasting. But God will know."

I'm afraid there's a whole subculture in our generation that wouldn't get Jesus' humor, because their capacity for laughter has been misshapen. Too much contemporary humor relies on shock and self-conscious naughtiness—the use of profanity, vulgarity, or the scatological. Some comedians get laughter, not because they've said something funny or insightful, but because they've used words on a public platform that ordinarily are heard (if at all) only in private speech.

We need Jesus the humorist. He would break through our pretentiousness and pomposity and force us to laugh at ourselves—and in the process, to change ourselves. Sometimes we need a new sense of dignity and self-worth, but just as surely, we sometimes need to laugh at ourselves. We harden under re-proof, but we soften under humor.

And we need to be reminded that laughter is more at home in the courts of holiness than in any other setting. Who has more reason to laugh than those who are right with God and who are seeking to bless the lives of others? As the late William Barclay said, "A gloomy Christian is a contradiction in terms" (*The Gospel of John,* vol. 2, 206). If I imagine having lunch or dinner with Jesus, I picture conversation in which laughter rolls in again and again—and with the laughter, a profound sense of the goodness of God and the ultimate gladness of life.

Some years ago Grenville Kleiser said that what this country needs is not a new national anthem, or a Wall Street boom, but the ability to laugh spontaneously. Spontaneous laughter is not, of itself, the product of humor, but those who live with laughter near the surface seem to find more reasons to laugh, and to see humor where others do not. Jesus brings that quality into life.

So if Jesus were among us today, would he be a humorist? Probably not as a full-time occupation. But if he followed the pattern of his first-century ministry, humor would mark his teaching, his social life, his daily relationships. He would cause great discomfort to religious leaders of both the right and the left, as he would probe past our professional religion and our self-centered piety. Struggling souls would realize that they had an advocate as he would turn humor to their defense. Children and teenagers would get his humor, and would laugh while some of us, trying hard to be properly serious, would miss what he was driving at.

He would cause politicians to sputter and fume as he would call for more than superficial commitment. I'd love to hear the figure of speech he might employ as he would uncover the hypocrisy of those public figures who live by a well-phrased sound byte. What incisive, biting word would he have for the scholar who is a good critic but who remains well above the pain he critiques? And how would our culture handle such humor? Would we grow as unhappy with it as the Pharisees did in their day? No doubt about it: by quick moments of humor he would make us examine our superficialities, while gently leading us to a higher way.

Jesus would reflect the thinking of the ancient wise man: "A cheerful heart is a good medicine" (Prov. 17:22). He would bring good cheer to life. As surely as, twenty centuries ago, children flocked to him and the dispossessed invited him to their parties, so in our time we would know he was present because we would hear laughter.

If you and I were more like Jesus, would there be more laughter wherever we go?

Study Questions

1. Who is your favorite humorist, either as a writer or a performer? How does your preference for this kind of humor influence your perception of Jesus as a humorist?
2. List some of the ways that humor of all kinds affects your daily life. What part does humor play in your Christian faith and life?
3. Read Matthew 6:25–7:5. What is the relationship between humor and trusting God? What connection, if any, do you see between laughter and faith? Is it possible really to trust God, yet have a morose personality?
4. Read Matthew 6:16-18. Have you ever known someone who seemed to feel that he or she proved his religion by a sober, painful manner? Have you at times been that kind of person yourself? Why are people sometimes so inclined to be "serious" when they're in church?
5. Dr. Elton Trueblood compiled a list of at least thirty instances in the Gospels where Jesus made a point by using humor. Can you identify one such instance? What can you learn from this?

Focus for the Week:
Laughter Belongs in Lent

Because Lent is a season of preparation and of sacrifice, we might easily forget that laughter is always appropriate to the Christian faith. If our laughter were of a superficial kind, or if—

like some humor—it depended on demeaning others, it would be inappropriate not only for this season but for all of life. But laughter belongs to the Christian faith as surely as do faith, hope, and healing. After all, who has more reason to laugh, and to feel deep-down hope, than those who trust in God?

This week, enjoy God's gift of laughter!

Jesus of Nazareth, Psychiatrist

Scripture Lesson: John 2:23–3:6

Our age is very self-conscious, so it isn't surprising that we have come up with many names for ourselves. I have a feeling that some future generation will finally describe us as "the age of psychiatry." We could make the case for such a label with a flurry of statistics, beginning with the fact that there are nearly forty thousand psychiatrists in the United States alone—and they are, so to speak, only the tip of the iceberg of psychologists and varieties of counselors. Consider that at least one-third of our hospital beds are occupied by the mentally ill, that many of our so-called street people ought to be hospitalized, and that multitudes are emotionally unable to cope with life.

The anecdotal evidence is even more impressive. For instance, browse for awhile at an airport or drugstore magazine stand. It's a rare periodical that doesn't carry some kind of feature story related to psychiatry, psychology, mental health, or personality development. Some magazines have a "resident counselor" on the staff, to answer questions in each issue about mental health and human relationships. Moreover, children sometimes begin psychiatric counseling before they enter kindergarten, and some families spend more on the mental health expert who is treating their pet than they do on their dentist or family practitioner.

I don't think we begin to realize how much the insights and vocabulary of psychiatry and human psychology pervade our daily lives. Our American ancestors salted their speech with the language of the Scriptures. We season ours with phrases and insights from psychiatry. Think how often you see, hear, or use such terms as *psychotic, neurotic, inferiority complex, depression, paranoia, schizophrenia,* or *personality disorder.* It's interesting, and a little frightening, to see how many of us practice psychiatry without a license! We've read a newspaper or magazine article about the human personality, and we quickly apply it to ourselves, our friends, or those we dislike. Some studies show that the language of psychology and psychiatry has become the preferred pulpit language for vast numbers of clergy of nearly every denomination, both liberal and conservative.

So I dare to suggest to our psychologically oriented age that if Jesus of Nazareth were physically present with us today, he might well be a psychiatrist. After all, how could he, who loved humanity so much, ignore such a prevalent need and concern? Especially when you remember that the word *psychiatry* comes from the Greek word *psyche,* which means "soul"? Who would be more likely to treat the illnesses of the soul than Jesus of Nazareth, the supreme doctor of the soul? And who could be more equipped to bring healing and wholeness to the soul than he?

The Gospel of John gives us a kind of thumbnail sketch of Jesus as psychiatrist when it says that he accepted the adulation of the crowds with caution, and that he "needed no one to testify about anyone; for he himself knew what was in everyone" (John 2:25). Several of the stories that then follow in John's Gospel show Jesus at work as a master psychiatrist, healing the human soul.

Take, for example, the story of Nicodemus (John 3). Here was a person of learning, achievement, and deep spirituality, yet he had hardly finished greeting Jesus before Jesus challenged him to be "born again," or "born from above." For all his achievements, Nicodemus was lacking something strategic, and Jesus put his finger on it. I wonder how many outstanding persons in our communities would get the same soul-analysis if Jesus were their psychiatrist? Despite all their achievements and honors, and with all that might be admirable in their character, they need something deeper, something best described as a new birth. Our soul sickness isn't always shown by erratic behavior or by a failure in our human relationships. I wonder how many outwardly attractive people are living in a way that Henry David

Thoreau described as "lives of quiet desperation"? They manage, by sheer strength of personality, to hold life together, but it is with unfulfilled longings, and without an abiding sense of purpose. I have a feeling that our dinner parties, our cruise ships, our sports arenas and concert halls are crowded with such souls. They need what only the Ultimate Psychiatrist can give; they need to be born again.

Consider also the unnamed woman in the fourth chapter of John's Gospel. She has been married five times and is now living with a man who is not her husband. Her life is a shambles. Jesus goes directly to her human need and tells her that she needs a drink of the water of life, which satisfies our deepest, eternal thirst. Jesus recognized the thirst in her life, just as he recognized the unnatural "aging" in the character of Nicodemus.

In these instances, typical of Jesus' whole ministry, he sought to restore the human personality to its full effectiveness. He believed that God means for us to live abundant lives, lives full of purpose and gladness. Whenever a human personality is limited or made less than it was created to be, a deliverance is needed. Jesus gave people the freedom to be what God meant them to be.

Jesus' healing was never superficial. He dared to deal with the root of our human need, the issue of sin. Dr. Paul Tournier recalls that when the Swiss psychiatrist Maeder of Zurich became a Christian, he said that he had been caring for people's souls for twenty years without seeing "the most important fact about the life of the soul—namely, sin" (*A Doctor's Casebook in the Light of the Bible*, 192). Karl Menninger, perhaps the most honored name in American psychiatry, put the issue squarely a few years ago by titling his book, *Whatever Became of Sin?* Any remedy that ignores the fact of sin will be a superficial remedy. Yet Jesus confronted our problem with a gracious word; he so often described us as lost—not a condemning word, but a compassionate one.

Perhaps Jesus never spoke a kinder word than one that some might consider a demanding one; indeed, it *was* demanding, and that was its kindness. When he had delivered an adulterous woman from her accusers, he sent her away with a gracious word, but also with an insistent one: "Go . . . and from now on do not sin again" (John 8:11). He gave the same warning to a man who had been healed of a paralysis that had bound him for thirty-eight years: "Do not sin any more, so that nothing worse happens to you" (John 5:14).

So many of our popular remedies seem to be only displacements. We cure a particular malady, only to see some new one break out—often worse than the original. Jesus might have had our problem in mind when he spoke of a person out of whom a devil had been cast, but who then lived an orderly but an "empty" life, so that eventually the original devil returned, and brought seven worse spirits with him (Matt. 12:43-45). When we have found health, we need to nurture that health; or, in the language of John's Gospel, when we have been born again, we need to grow up. A new life, even one born from above, must have some direction and purpose, or it will eventually fail of its potential; indeed, its very potential may be turned against itself.

Jesus would be such a remarkable psychiatrist if he were with us today! Those who truly wanted healing would flock to him, probably crossing all kinds of boundaries and overcoming every difficulty to seek his aid. They would find a psychiatrist of extraordinary compassion, yet one who would never deceive them in a foolish effort to protect their feelings. They would find him insistent and demanding: "I can't leave you just healed and contented," he would say. "Now you must begin to grow. You must become *perfect*, as your Father in heaven is perfect. You were meant to live abundantly, and I won't be happy with you until you reach such a level of daily fullness." We would leave our hour with him knowing that he had looked into our very soul, and that he had seen not only what we are, but more wondrously, what God has intended us to be. If I am honest, I must add that some patients would forsake Jesus for another doctor. They would find his prescriptions too demanding and his passion for their health too confining. They would look for an easier practitioner—perhaps one who would let them remain a little bit sick!

Of course, Jesus' greatest gift as a psychiatrist would not be in his diagnosis, nor in his prescription, but simply in himself. To be with Jesus is to be exposed to true wholeness. He who wanted only to do God's will was so engaged with that will that those who touched him caught some measure of the same passion.

Those who met Jesus, twenty centuries ago, were made whole not simply because his ideas and insights were right and powerful, but because he inspired new dreams and new resolves—and gave others the power to achieve them.

The ultimate wonder is this: his power still touches our lives in such transforming ways today. He is the Great Physician of the human soul, and even the spread of the centuries has not diminished his power.

Study Questions

1. In what ways are your thinking and conversation influenced by psychology and psychiatry? Do you think these topics have become unduly emphasized in our time?
2. Read John 3. If you had known Nicodemus, do you think you would have seen anything in his personality that needed correction? Is it fair to feel that something was lacking in his life? If not, why would Jesus have insisted that he needed to be born again? Is it possible to be morally good, yet to be unfulfilled, and to be living an empty life?
3. Read John 4. Are we minimizing the sinful nature of this woman's conduct by suggesting that she needed healing for her "thirst"? Suppose she had lived a morally responsible life, but still was suffering from the kind of thirst that is revealed in her conversation with Jesus; would she still need a Savior—the "living water" of which Jesus spoke? Or would her moral conduct have been enough?
4. When we speak of someone growing in faith, what connection do you see between holiness and wholeness?

Focus for the Week:
Lent Is a Time of Wholeness

Lent is so often seen as a time when we "give up" some food or practice that we may find it difficult to see it for what it is: a season in which we are led to true wholeness. Life outside of Christ is always incomplete; the more "saved" we are, the more whole we will be. The better our relationship with God, the better will be our relationships with others and with the totality of life. To grow in Christ is to become more truly whole.

If you were to spend one hour with Jesus the psychiatrist this week, what soul-analysis would he give you?

Jesus of Nazareth, Executive

Scripture Lesson: Luke 10:1-12

For several generations Americans said proudly that the secret of American progress was our "know-how," our management skills. When the Germans and the Japanese began to compete with America's standards, we acknowledged that those countries had such skills, too. Vast natural resources and a hospitable climate are not enough to make a nation prosper; there must also be the ability to organize those resources and advantages so that they are not wasted.

The importance of management skills certainly is not limited to the business world. Is it significant, for example, that a baseball team is led by a *manager?* And isn't it interesting that when a sports writer described John Wooden, perhaps the greatest college basketball coach of all time, he referred to his "amazing sports *organization*"? Most of us probably feel that spirit is the most important element in a religious organization, yet it's clear that John Wesley's phenomenal contribution to church history came not through his preaching, but through his skill as an organizer and leader. His contemporary, George Whitefield, was a much more powerful preacher, but left nothing measurable behind, while Wesley's executive skills gave us the world Methodist movement.

So let me attach an unfamiliar title to Jesus; let me call him an *executive.* Are you uncomfortable with that term? If, like me, you love to picture Jesus as the small-town carpenter who lived a simple life among the common people, you may back off from a Jesus who would be at home in the executive suite. But don't carry the imagery too far. I'm not thinking about an executive lifestyle, but about management skills. And when it comes to management skills, Jesus got a high rating from someone who was in a position to know.

It happened when a centurion came to Jesus on behalf of his sick servant. Centurions were not simply army officers; they were the key element in what may have been the most efficient administration history has ever seen: the Roman Empire. In an era of primitive communication, the Romans managed to hold together a vast mass of widely dissimilar peoples, while they built a structure that has never been surpassed.

One of the key administrators in this system, a centurion, came to Jesus for help. When Jesus prepared to accompany him to his home, the centurion answered that it wasn't necessary for him to do so. He explained that he was himself a man under authority who also exercised authority over others—that is, he was someone who understood executive orders, who dealt daily with a chain of command. He saw Jesus as one of his own kind, an executive who could give a command and make it stick. He was envisioning Jesus as an *executive*—what our culture might call "a take-charge type" (Matt. 8:5-13). It's interesting that the Gospel of Mark, which is often seen as being aimed originally at the Romans, is characterized by the Greek word *eutheos,* a word that is translated "straightway" or "immediately." Jesus is portrayed as someone who acted decisively. He was "in command."

The common folk saw Jesus' executive personality at another level. As they watched him heal the sick and take command of the violently insane, they declared that he had such "authority" that he could command even the unclean spirits (Mark 1:27). They had seen the Roman soldiers exercise authority in subduing unruly mobs; they recognized the same executive power in the way Jesus handled irrational spirits.

All the disciples had their own stories, I'm sure, about Jesus' executive power, but no one more than Matthew. He was sitting one day at his customs table, collecting taxes. Matthew was a "bottom-line" kind of man, who knew his business and probably reveled in it. But when Jesus stopped and said simply, "Follow me," Matthew got up and followed. The Gospel writer spares the details, but it's clear that something in Jesus' manner was irresistible. He was an executive, exuding authority without a hint of manipulation.

The words we usually associate with an executive are *organization* and *administration*. Let me show you Jesus at work in a setting where many executives might wilt under the threat. A great crowd had been with Jesus so long that they couldn't get to their homes before dark, and they were hungry. A hungry mob is dangerous! When the disciples explained the predicament to Jesus, he asked them how many loaves they had. That is, take an inventory. You never know what you can do until you find out what your resources really are. Unfortunately, the inventory gave them little reason to hope; they had only five loaves and two fish.

So Jesus did an administrative thing. He had them seat the people on the green grass, in groups of hundreds and fifties. Thus he turned the mob into an orderly company. If I had been there, I would have been reassured by this strong action. And note that I said Jesus seated them in the *green grass*. That was a significant psychological move. Earlier the setting is described as a lonely place; the King James Version calls it "a desert place." But Jesus had the people seated in what little green area could be found—an act that would change the mood of the people.

Then Jesus proceeded to break the few loaves and fish and give them to the disciples to distribute; and as he did, the multitudes were fed. When the meal was completed, Jesus made another management decision: he asked the disciples to pick up the leftovers—twelve baskets full. We read this story as the record of a miracle; but the miracle happens in a scene of superior administration. Without such administration—simple, preliminary measures—I wonder if the miracle might ever have taken place.

We see this same administrative quality at work in the scripture that forms the basis of this lesson. Jesus was sending out seventy missioners. Incidentally, this was itself an executive act. A key executive rule is to enlist good coworkers; great jobs can't be done as grand solos. But brief as the story is, see how carefully Jesus set up the project. He didn't say, "Go wherever you feel led, stay where you want, and as long as you want." Instead, he gave specific rules of conduct and procedure. It was an organized, highly disciplined operation. It had to be, if it were going to work.

Of course, the crucial measure of an executive comes at the time of crisis, in the lonely hour of the hard decision. Abraham Lincoln said that there are times when a president cannot lay the burden of decision on his cabinet; there are times, as General Eisenhower discovered on his lonely walk on the night before D day, when the leader must carry the final responsibility. So it was with Jesus. As tension mounted in the last months of his ministry, he knew there would be a showdown if he went to Jerusalem for the Passover. So what did he do? He "set his face" to go to Jerusalem (Luke 9:51). He made a final, hard executive decision, knowing that it would bring judgment, abuse, and death.

Above all, Jesus was a master executive in his dealings with people, especially in the way he invested *time* in people—not only the disciples who would carry on his work, but people in general, all kinds of people. He gave time to people who in that culture—and often in ours—are easily ignored: children and women, the poor, the physically distressed, the social outcasts. He operated on the principle that nothing is as important as human beings. The truly great executives all learn this principle, and those who forget it lose their executive touch.

Jesus did an impossible thing, against all odds. He gathered around himself a group of small businessmen and tax collectors who could never hope to be more than that. There is no evidence of executive or leadership skills in them. Yet he molded them into an organization, which, within that century, would carry his message into the then-known world. They would become the foundation for an institution that exists two thousand years later in every part of the world. Not one of the disciples was, by our usual measure, a notable success; before his call, not one was known beyond his own little village. Yet Jesus, the master executive, developed them into a force that eventually challenged the Roman Empire.

Jesus was an executive, no doubt about it. Without office or fanfare, without the benefit of inherited authority or public endorsement, he produced results that ought to elicit a gasp of surprise from this century of ours, which believes executive skill is a science.

We need his executive gifts today. To run the churches that bear his name, yes; but also to infuse new gifts of human concern and dignity in the executive suite and in the halls of government.

Above all, we need him to run our individual lives. Perhaps there is no better figure of speech to describe Christian conversion than to see it as a change in management. That's what we need, you and I, if we are to avoid ultimate personal bankruptcy. We need a new chief executive: Jesus of Nazareth.

Study Questions

1. What executive skills do you use in your daily work? Does any one of us do work in which *no* executive skills are needed?
2. Read Matthew 14:13-21. Do you agree that the details in this story are so significant? If they are not, why are they included in the story? Do you feel that the crowds responded, consciously or unconsciously, to Jesus' acts of leadership?
3. Read Luke 10:1-12. Compare Jesus' organizing of the seventy with the way your own church is organized for mission. The situations are different, of course, but would any of Jesus' rules apply to a local congregation, at least in principle? Do we have a clear idea of what our local congregation should be doing?
4. In practical terms, why must an executive be so sensitive to the capabilities of people?

Focus for the Week: Lent Is a Time for Leadership

Jesus calls us to follow him, and when we do so, we become leaders, because our lives then become examples for others. Lent is a season for developing the qualities within which make for truly courageous and honorable leadership. Consider the many areas where leadership is needed: in the home, in service clubs, in school, in community organizations, in neighborhood responsibility, in city, state, and nation. Are we Christians providing the kind of leadership that can rightfully be expected of persons who follow the Great Executive? In what ways is Jesus calling you to be a leader? What skills or qualities do you need to develop or improve?

Jesus of Nazareth, Ph.D.

Scripture Lesson: Matthew 7:24-29

Once again I've given Jesus a title that may trouble you. It's not that I intend to be difficult; but it's a problem, you see, to catapult Jesus from the first century to the twentieth century. Common terms take on new definitions, and new definitions can be uncomfortable.

In a sense, nothing could be more logical than to identify Jesus as a Doctor of Philosophy. After all, if there was a single title that Jesus' contemporaries attached to him, it was *Teacher*. We refer to him often as "the greatest Teacher that ever lived." Well, since our culture looks upon the Ph.D. degree as the highest basic attainment in education, why not give that designation to Jesus?

Our discomfort may be partly because the modern Ph.D. represents highly specialized learning. The areas of human knowledge have become so vast that a scholar cannot hope to cover the whole of even a major field. For instance, a student of history doesn't try to cover all of history, or even all of American history. Instead, he or she specializes in some single phase of American history, such as military, cultural, or intellectual history; or perhaps a single period, such as the colonial period, or the nineteenth century following the Civil War. Well, that kind of scholarship just doesn't seem to fit Jesus. We can't imagine him becoming party to the academic rat race, caught up in the "publish or perish" mood, preparing esoteric papers for a professional journal. Such work has its place and its worth, but it doesn't seem to fit Jesus of Nazareth, the Teacher.

And yet there's no doubt that our times call for a master teacher. Never in human history has the store of knowledge accumulated as rapidly as in our day. Scientific and technical literature is being published at the rate of tens of millions of pages annually. It is said that when a child born today is fifty years old, 97 percent of everything we know about the world will have been learned since the time he or she was born. On the one hand, such a statement is misleading, because the basic knowledge remains somewhat the same. But the statistic does indicate, fairly enough, the astonishing proliferation of new data.

At the same time, we are increasingly disillusioned about education. It hasn't brought the perfect world we anticipated. Someone asked Albert Speer, Hitler's close associate, who later became the author of two best-selling books on the Nazi era, how a person of his intelligence could allow himself to be part of a system as evil as Nazism. Speer answered that there is, unfortunately, "no necessary correlation between intelligence and decency"; the genius and the moron, he continued, "are equally susceptible to corruption." Sometimes it seems that the more people know, the better equipped they are to do harm. Furthermore, increased learning does not necessarily bring greater happiness or fulfillment in life. The American Psychoanalytic Association reports that most patients who seek help are highly educated.

So we need a teacher. Call him a doctor of philosophy, but be sure it is a life-giving philosophy. We need a teacher, not to offer an arcane insight about some obscure literary passage, but to equip us to live our lives with dignity and with eternal promise.

Nineteen centuries ago they called Jesus "Teacher." The common people made him their particular property, hearing him gladly and exulting in the way he exceeded the usual teachers of their time. But even a member of the nation's most prestigious intellectual and religious body said to him, "Rabbi, we know that you are a teacher who has come from God" (John 3:2).

Yet Jesus' style of teaching was quite different from what we would expect today. He didn't convene classes in a building, teach courses with an academic number, or require semester exams and term papers. At first, he taught often in the synagogues, the conventional learning center of the Jewish community. Any member of a congregation, or even a visitor, was able to do so. But then he began to do more and more of his teaching in the streets and along the lakeshore. Almost any place could become a classroom: a hillside became the setting for what we call the Sermon on the Mount; a boat, pushed just off from the shore, became a podium; a dusty highway between Jerusalem and Jericho, a village well in Samaria, a street corner in Jerusalem, a little home in Bethany—wherever people gathered around him, he taught.

Perhaps the main thing that made his teaching so appealing was that the people could understand him. Some teachers are so anxious to impress students with their learning that they frustrate the students' own ability to learn; on the other hand, some teachers become so absorbed in their subject that they lose contact with those they are trying to teach. Not Jesus. His students could understand him. He told them stories: a certain man had two sons, he said, and one of them wanted his inheritance early. The crowd pricked up their ears to hear what happened. A farmer sowed his fields, he said, but one night an enemy came and sowed weeds in the midst of the grain. In such fashion he talked with the crowds about the world they knew and led them into an understanding of truths they had never before been able to grasp.

But there was another reason Jesus' teaching was so appealing; it was the *authority* in his teaching. The people were astonished, Mark says, because Jesus taught them as one who had authority, and not as the scribes (Mark 1:22). Mark says that the people in Jesus' home town marveled at his wisdom, wondering where he had got such insight (Mark 6:2). What, indeed, made Jesus different? To use the language of scholarship, Jesus was different because he had done so much primary research. The scribes, who were praiseworthy in their earnestness, worked with secondary sources; they studied what other teachers had written about God and life and humanity. But Jesus went to the primary source; he spoke out of his own profound communion with the Father. Mind you, he knew the books; thus in his days of temptation in the wilderness, he could answer the tempter with the language of scripture. But he had the authority of one who had worked with the facts firsthand.

On the basis of that authority, Jesus said some daring things. You can either take them or leave them, but Jesus doesn't leave you any room to compromise. In the Sermon on the Mount, Jesus said that those who follow his teachings are like a person who builds on a rock, while those who ignore his teachings are like one who builds on the sand, where life can so easily be washed away (Matt. 7:24-29). He said that he is the way, the truth, and the life (John 14:6)—audacious words unless he could back them up.

As the late E. Stanley Jones put it, everything Jesus taught, he embodied. No wonder the Gospel of John says of Jesus that "the Word became flesh and lived among us" (John 1:14). That's the kind of Teacher we need! We have heard all the great words; now we need to see them. We have *heard* of truth and grace and love, but we need to see them in action.

That is, Jesus was not only the Teacher, he was also the Lesson. Others had told of the goodness and mercy of God, but he became the embodiment of those qualities. As they looked at him, it was as if God had stepped out of the frame of the universe, full of grace and truth.

What a Teacher! An English poet has said that the cross was Jesus' "professorial chair." In the world of education, there are endowed "chairs" to which esteemed educators are appointed. Such a chair is a position of authority, adding to the prestige of the teacher. So see the chair from which Jesus teaches: it is an instrument of torture and destruction, stark and ugly on a hill. Of itself it is a repulsive sight; a stumbling block, as Paul called it.

But Jesus has made the cross a chair of esteem. Other teachers are made more notable by the chair to which they are appointed. Jesus was assigned to a place of shame, and he transformed it into an emblem of majesty. A world, destitute of learning, moves restlessly around the chair of the teacher, half scornful, half embarrassed. What could anyone teach from such a discrediting spot as this?

Jesus spoke few words from the cross, but his lessons were unforgettable; they pursue us two thousand years later. To a world that says, "There's a coldness at the heart of the universe," Jesus answers from the cross, "Not a coldness, but an unceasing love. You may think you hear the pounding of nails in a gibbet, but it is the beating of the heart of God."

What a Teacher! Raised in a hill country town, trained by his mother and a village rabbi, he knew nothing of Rome or Athens or Alexandria. His students were the simplest folk in the land. And when at last they gave him a professorial chair, it was a cross. But he was, and is, such a teacher that the world continues to bow before him at that cross. And I am ready, myself, to enroll again in his class!

Study Questions

1. What image comes to your mind with the term, "Ph.D."? How does this fit your conception of Jesus?
2. Compare and contrast Jesus' style and setting of teaching with education as you have experienced it. Are they so different as to be beyond comparison? What basic matters remain the same?
3. Read Matthew 7:24-29. Does it seem arrogant of Jesus to speak so emphatically of the power of his own teachings? As you contemplate our contemporary culture and its popular philosophies, give some examples of "sand foundations" on which people currently build.
4. Read John 14:6. Try to give a short definition of way, truth, and life. In what sense does Jesus fit your definitions? When Jesus said, "No one comes to the Father except through me," how "exclusive" is this intended to be? Is salvation still being offered to the whole human race?

Focus for the Week:
Lent Is a Time of Learning

When we become Christians, we set out on a lifelong pilgrimage of learning. But it is learning of a very special kind; I think we might rightly call it *transformational learning*. It is not simply a matter of accumulating more knowledge, but of taking knowledge to ourselves in such a way that our lives are changed. That is why the Christian faith is a life of growth. Each day we are expected to learn, and therefore to grow, and therefore to change. Lent is a season particularly dedicated to this experience. By its very structure and emphasis, it is intended to help us grow and be transformed.

What new lessons or insights have you gained this season? This week? How have you grown or changed as a result?

Seventh Week in Lent

Jesus of Nazareth, Cosmic Personality

Scripture Lesson: Colossians 1:15-23

How unbelievably our world has changed in this twentieth century! As the century began, the automobile was such a rare sight that people ran out to see one pass. When Ransom Olds manufactured 425 gas engine models in 1901, it was hailed as an achievement in mass production. Some two or three years later, the Wright brothers of North Carolina flew their little airplane 120 feet. Today we are almost casual about exploratory trips to the moon, and we take it for granted that satellites give us constant reports from outer space.

Most of our grandparents or great-grandparents thought of their neighborhood as a block or two in town, or the few farms adjoining theirs. The next generation talked of visiting another state. We speak just as naturally of traveling abroad. It is possible that our children will take package tours to another planet. When our grandparents or great-grandparents worried about how their decisions might affect their neighbors, they worried that the disposal from the outhouse might seep into the rock at a level where it could contaminate water for a neighbor down the hill. Nowadays we worry that a bomb that is tested ten thousand miles from here may someday drop its pollutants in our yard, and that some of our common household chemical usage may eat up the thinning ozone layer.

After living for thousands of years in a kind of one-story world, we suddenly find that we are really part of a cosmic universe. Where once we looked for leaders who could manage affairs for a few thousand or a few million people, now it looks as if we need someone who can hold together the whole fabric of this vast creation.

. We are now part of the cosmic age, and we need a cosmic leader to fit it. So I offer you Jesus of Nazareth, the Cosmic Personality. In a sense this age, more than any other, is the one for which Jesus came.

That statement may startle you; you may even conclude that I am being naive, or that I'm just carried away. After all, it's easy to think of Jesus as a great teacher and a towering figure of human history, but the idea of a cosmic personality is quite beyond our usual imagining. You have thought with me as I have described Jesus in our twentieth-century world as a physician, a psychiatrist, an executive, and a news analyst, but it's quite another thing to think of him as a figure in a cosmic age. We needed imagination to see Jesus in those other roles; we need faith to see him in this one.

And yet the New Testament gives us more basis for this description than for any of the others I have ventured. Consider the way Jesus is introduced to us in the Gospel of John. Whereas Matthew and Luke tell the story from the vantage point of Bethlehem—when Caesar Augustus was in Rome, Herod was King of Judea, and Quirinius was governor of Syria (details that located the event at a time and place in the life of our planet)—John broadens the stage to the universe, and the time factor to eternity. "In the beginning was the Word, and the Word was with God, and the Word was God. He was in the beginning with God. All things came into being through him, and without him not one thing came into being. What has come into being in him was life, and the life was the light of all people" (John 1:1-4). Then, to tell of Jesus' birth, John says, "And the Word became flesh and lived among us" (John 1:14). John is telling us the same story as Matthew and Luke, but where those two writers viewed the story from a hillside in the village of Bethlehem, John saw it from the outer reaches of the universe. Malcolm Muggeridge, the British television personality, said simply, "The universe provides a stage; Jesus is the play" (Malcolm Muggeridge, *Jesus*, 17).

The cosmic plot that was revealed at Jesus' birth is suggested again as he was dying. Luke reminds us that on Good Friday "darkness came over the whole land," lasting from about noon until three in the afternoon and that "the sun's light failed" (Luke 23:44, 45). It is as if Luke wants us to know that the universe was responding to the event at Calvary, because it was a cosmic event.

We are so enchanted by the simple beauty of the Christmas story as Matthew and Luke tell it that we hardly hear the story when John tells it. And we are so taken with the details of our Lord's physical suffering at Calvary that we can easily miss the larger significance that the Gospel writers themselves see as the point of the whole story. It's no wonder, then, that we go through passage after passage in the epistles without ever being challenged by their awesome wonder.

Consider, for instance, what the apostle says in the Letter to the Colossians, that Jesus is "the image of the invisible God, the firstborn of all creation" (Col. 1:15). This is infinitely more than a picture of a first-century teacher in Galilee; indeed, it pales any scene we might imagine when we try to translate Jesus into twentieth-century terms, with the language of psychiatry, business, or the news media. The Jesus who is portrayed in the epistles and in John's Gospel is a cosmic personality, whose roots are before creation.

For, as Paul explains it, it is in Christ that "all things in heaven and on earth were created"—not only the things we can see, but even those "invisible" things, which the apostle describes as thrones, dominions, rulers, and powers (Col. 1:16). Jesus of Nazareth is Lord of the space age. He is ready for our times, and ahead of them. He is eternity's Cosmic Personality.

You and I can find great hope in this fact. The apostle said, "He himself is before all things, and in him all things hold together" (Col. 1:17). With the unleashing of atomic and hydrogen power and the developing of chemical properties that might destroy our planet, our pundits wonder if our earth can endure. Here is a reassuring word: all things cohere in Christ. There is a power holding the universe together, and it is the One who brought it into existence. Whatever the perils of these uncertain times, there are resources upon which we can draw. "In him all things hold together."

And that's not all. Paul says that through Christ "God was pleased to reconcile to himself all things, whether on earth or in heaven, by making peace through the blood of his cross" (Col. 1:20).

Ours is a badly fractured world, whether one speaks of the tensions between nations and ideologies or the bitterness that exists under the roofs of our homes; whether the issue is war or rancor or divorce, we are in need of peace. Sometimes one gets the feeling that something is out of line at the very heart of the universe itself. Why else would discord be woven so pervasively through life? Clearly enough, we need Someone who can touch life at its universal center; we need a Cosmic Christ.

What a word this is for Easter! From our human vantage point, death is the essence of all that is evil. All other human struggles seem tied to this one. "Where there's life, there's hope," we say, which is our acknowledgment that we can manage almost anything as long as we can hold death at bay. It's no wonder, then, that we keep trying to push back the boundaries of death, with a new cure, a miracle drug, or a better method of surgery. But with all our discoveries and marvels, we know we are not defeating death, we are only postponing its eventual victory.

But it is more than that. We want life not only to be longer; we also want it to be deeper and fuller. And with that we recognize that the principle of death shows itself not only in the termination of life, but also in the frustrating of life. One of the subtle expressions of death is in the way we fail to enjoy life even when we have it, or the way we waste it. That's why death is the worst enemy; it takes life from us not only in a final, dramatic act, but in endless little rearguard attacks, often so subtle that we hardly know they're happening.

That's why we need Easter. And when we speak of Easter, we're speaking of a Cosmic Christ. Easter calls for more than a philosopher, a teacher, or a doctor; we need more than good advice and sound opinions. We need Someone who can move with authority across the boundary between this world and the next, and between the known and the unknown.

We often say that only Easter can explain how the few scattered followers of a regional, crucified Teacher could become a worldwide institution. But if Easter explains the unique power of Christianity, what explains Easter?

The answer is Jesus Christ. Jesus of Nazareth was like no other personality in human history. He was God's once-for-all invasion into our human scene, God's answer to our need. Easter doesn't explain Jesus; Jesus explains Easter.

That's why we call Jesus of Nazareth the Cosmic Christ.

Study Questions

1. What images come to your mind with the word *cosmic?* Have you ever associated this word with Jesus Christ? Do you find it hard to do so? Can you think of a synonym that you might find more acceptable?
2. Read John 1:1-14. Do you think of this passage as part of the Christmas story, as surely as you do the stories in Matthew and Luke? Why don't we refer to this passage more often at Christmas time? Do you think we have ignored it partly because it doesn't have the sentimental attractiveness of the manger, the wise men, and the shepherds?
3. Read Colossians 1:15-19. Compare these verses with the passage you have just read in John. How many parallels or similarities can you find?
4. Read Colossians 1:20. List some areas of your life where reconciliation is needed.

Focus for the Week:
Lent Leads Us to Easter

Lent should never be seen as an end in itself. Its purpose is to prepare us for Easter. Lent is by nature a period of repentance, and often, therefore, of sorrow, as we contemplate our sins and our failure to be all that God has called us to be. But we ought not remain in that place; repentance is meant to lead us into the experience of forgiveness, and from there into the place of rejoicing. If we come to Easter without Lent and its experience of repentance, our Easter will be shallow and powerless; but if our Easter journey stops with the mood of Lent, we will fail to apprehend Easter's victory and joy.

How does thinking of Jesus as the Cosmic Christ influence or change your understanding of Easter? How can you make the joy of Easter part of your daily experience?